P9-CQK-004

SISTERS make the best friends

A Little Book of Quotations

PUBLISHED BY HISTORY & HERALDRY

History & Heraldry Ltd
Rotherham S66 8HR U.K.

I'm smiling
because
I'm your sister,
I'm laughing
because there's
nothing you
can do about it!

A sister shares
the memories of
yesterday, the
joys of today
and the hopes
of tomorrow.

I, who have no sisters, look with some degree of innocent envy on those who may be said to be born to friends.

J Boswell

The great gift of family
life is to be intimately
acquainted with people
you might never even
introduce yourself to,
had life not done it
for you.

Kendall Hailey

Other things may change us, but we start and end with family.

Anthony Brandt

A sister is
someone who
never lets you
forget all the
crazy things you
did in your life.

We laugh, we cry, we make time fly. Best friends are we, my sister and me.

There is nothing
quite like the
cherished love of
one who is both a
sister and a friend.

A lucky few,
have a sister
like you.

16

If at first you
don't succeed,
try to hide your
astonishment.

17

A woman is like a teabag. You never know how strong she is until you put her in hot water.

A sister is a
special part, of
all that's
cherished in the
heart.

19

Big sisters are the crab grass in the lawn of life.

Charles M Schultz
'Peanuts' 1952

Personally, I think if a woman hasn't met the right man by the time she's 24, she may be lucky.

Deborah Kerr

Sisterly love is,
of all sentiments, the
most abstract.
Nature does not grant
it any functions.

Ugo Betti

Sometimes when
one person is missing,
the whole world
seems depopulated.

Men seldom
make passes,

At girls who
wear glasses.

But a girl on a sofa,

Is easily won ofa.

Dorothy Parker

You don't know a
woman until you've
had a letter from her.

Ada Leverson

It's the good girls who keep diaries; the bad girls never have time.

Tallulah Bankhead
American actress

My sister! My sweet
sister! If a name
Dearer and purer were,
it should be thine.

Lord Byron

Children are natural
mimics. They act like
their parents in spite of
every attempt to teach
them good manners.

Anon

Heredity is a splendid phenomenon that relieves us of responsibility for our shortcomings.

Doug Larson

When our relatives
are at home, we have
to think of all their
good points or it
would be impossible
to endure them.

George Bernard Shaw

The thing women
have got to learn is
that nobody gives
you power.
You just take it.

Roseanne Barr

Though men are
brothers their pockets
are not sisters.

Turkish proverb

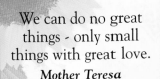

We can do no great
things - only small
things with great love.

Mother Teresa

There is no friend
like a sister
In calm or stormy
weather;
To cheer one on the
tedious way,
To fetch one if

one goes astray,
To lift one if one
totters down,
To strengthen whilst
one stands.

Christina Rossetti

One would be in
less danger
From the whiles of
the stranger
If one's own kin
and kith
Were more fun to be with.

Ogden Nash

From birth to age 18 a girl needs good parents. From 18 to 35 she needs good looks. From 35 to 55 she

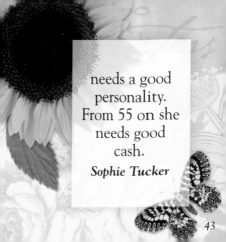

needs a good
personality.
From 55 on she
needs good
cash.

Sophie Tucker

43

I can do
without
essentials, but
I must have
luxuries.

Anon

Are there any brothers who do not criticise a bit and make fun of the fiancé who is stealing a sister from them?

Colette

We tell the ladies that
good wives make
good husbands;
I believe it is a more
certain position that
good brothers make
good sisters.

Samuel Johnson

Blood's thicker than
water,
And when one's in
trouble
Best to seek out a
relative's open arms.

Euripides
'Aromache Lamartine'

Reproof a parent's
province is; A sister's
discipline is this:
By studied kindness
to effect
A little brother's
young respect.

Mary Lamb

Never praise a
sister to a sister,
in the hope
of your
compliments
reaching the
proper ears.

51

An ounce of
blood is worth
more than a
pound of
friendship.

Spanish proverb

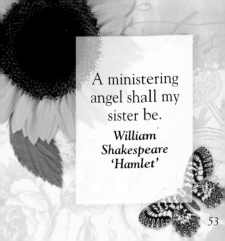

A ministering
angel shall my
sister be.

*William
Shakespeare
'Hamlet'*

The family - that dear
octopus form whose
tentacles we never
quite escape.

Dodie Smith
'Dear Octopus'

God grant me the
serenity to accept
the things I cannot
change, courage
to change the
things I can,

and wisdom to
always tell the
difference.

Kurt Vonnegut
'Slaughterhouse-Five'

I am treating you as my friend, asking you to share my present minuses in the hope that I can ask you to share my future pluses.

Katherine Mansfield

Remember that no one can make you feel inferior without your consent.

Eleanor Roosevelt

There's no
friend like a
sister, and no
sister quite
like you.

61